PRINCEWILL LAGANG

Mastering Luxury: The Bernard Arnault Chronicles

First published by PRINCEWILL LAGANG 2023

First edition

This book was professionally typeset on Reedsy.
Find out more at reedsy.com

Contents

1

Introduction

The introduction serves as the gateway into the captivating narrative of "Mastering Luxury: The Bernard Arnault Chronicles." It immerses readers into the extraordinary world of luxury, setting the stage for the exploration of Bernard Arnault's remarkable journey. From the early days of Arnault's life to the formation of LVMH Moët Hennessy Louis Vuitton, this introduction offers a glimpse into the visionary leadership and strategic acumen that have shaped the evolution of luxury under Arnault's guidance. As readers embark on this narrative, they are invited to witness the convergence of tradition and innovation, the resilience in the face of challenges, and the indelible mark left by Arnault on the timeless canvas of opulence.

2

The Genesis of Genius

Title: "Mastering Luxury: The Bernard Arnault Chronicles"

In the heart of the bustling metropolis of Paris, where the Seine River weaves through centuries of history, a tale of visionary entrepreneurship and unparalleled success begins. This is the story of Bernard Arnault, a man whose name has become synonymous with luxury, innovation, and the relentless pursuit of excellence.

The year was 1949 when Bernard Jean Étienne Arnault was born into a modest family with roots deeply embedded in the French business landscape. As the second of five children, Arnault's early years were shaped by a blend of familial values and the ethos of post-war reconstruction. Little did the world know that within this unassuming boy, a relentless passion for business and an unwavering commitment to craftsmanship were beginning to take root.

The opening chapter of "Mastering Luxury: The Bernard Arnault Chronicles" unravels the formative years that laid the foundation for Arnault's future empire. Raised with a keen awareness of business by his father, Jean Leon Arnault, Bernard learned the ropes from a young age. His early exposure to the construction and property development industry provided him with valuable insights into strategic thinking and the art of deal-making.

As he matured, Arnault's ambitions expanded beyond the realm of his family's enterprises. A brilliant student with a voracious appetite for knowledge, he entered the École Polytechnique, one of France's most prestigious engineering schools. This academic journey, marked by rigor and discipline, not only honed his analytical skills but also instilled in him the ability to navigate complex challenges—an attribute that would prove indispensable in the competitive world of luxury.

Upon completing his studies, Arnault pivoted towards the family business, gradually asserting his leadership and shaping it to reflect his own aspirations. The narrative unfolds against the backdrop of the 1970s, a period of economic turbulence that would test Arnault's acumen and resilience. It was during this time that he demonstrated an innate ability to identify opportunities amid adversity, marking the inception of his ascent in the business world.

"Mastering Luxury" takes readers on a captivating journey through Arnault's early forays into the world of luxury goods. From the acquisition of Boussac, a struggling textile empire, to the audacious takeover of iconic French fashion house Christian Dior, each move was a carefully orchestrated step towards a grander vision. Arnault's strategic brilliance and the meticulous execution of his plans positioned him as a trailblazer in an industry where tradition often clashed with innovation.

The opening chapter concludes with the emergence of Arnault as a formidable force in the luxury sector. His journey from a young, ambitious entrepreneur to a shaper of global taste and style sets the stage for the subsequent chapters, where the narrative will delve into the evolution of LVMH Moët Hennessy Louis Vuitton—the conglomerate that stands as a testament to Bernard Arnault's indomitable spirit and unparalleled mastery of luxury.

3

The Birth of LVMH

Title: "Redefining Luxury: The LVMH Moët Hennessy Louis Vuitton Saga"

As the 1980s dawned, the world witnessed the meteoric rise of Bernard Arnault as a transformative figure in the realm of luxury. Chapter 2 of "Mastering Luxury: The Bernard Arnault Chronicles" delves into the pivotal period that saw the formation of LVMH Moët Hennessy Louis Vuitton—a conglomerate that would redefine the very essence of luxury and establish Arnault as a visionary tycoon.

The chapter opens with the acquisition of Boussac, a move that not only rescued the failing conglomerate but also laid the groundwork for Arnault's grand ambitions. His strategic vision went beyond the traditional boundaries of luxury, encompassing a diverse portfolio that included not only fashion but also champagne, cognac, and perfumes. Arnault's audacity to envision a luxury empire that spanned a myriad of industries set the stage for the creation of LVMH.

The narrative unravels the intricacies of Arnault's calculated approach to assembling a portfolio of prestigious brands. The acquisition of iconic names such as Givenchy, Kenzo, and Hennessy positioned LVMH as a powerhouse with an unparalleled influence on global luxury markets. The chapter explores Arnault's unique management style, characterized by a delicate balance between nurturing creativity and maintaining rigorous financial discipline.

A central theme in this chapter is Arnault's visionary move to integrate his acquisitions, creating synergies that transcended individual brands. The formation of LVMH marked a departure from the conventional approach to luxury conglomerates, as Arnault sought to foster an environment where each brand retained its distinctive identity while benefiting from the collective strength of the group.

The narrative also illuminates the challenges Arnault faced during this transformative period. Skepticism and resistance from the traditionalists within the industry were met with Arnault's unwavering determination to modernize and innovate. His foresight to recognize the potential of emerging markets, particularly in Asia, further solidified LVMH's global dominance.

As the chapter unfolds, readers witness the birth of a new era in luxury—a paradigm where craftsmanship, creativity, and business acumen converged under the umbrella of LVMH. Bernard Arnault's ability to navigate the delicate balance between tradition and modernity, coupled with his innate understanding of consumer desires, positioned him as a true master of luxury.

Chapter 2 sets the stage for the subsequent chapters, where the narrative will explore LVMH's continued expansion, the integration of additional iconic brands, and Arnault's enduring commitment to setting the standard for excellence in the ever-evolving world of luxury.

4

The Art of Curation

Title: "Curating Dreams: Bernard Arnault's Mastery in Luxury Brand Management"

As LVMH Moët Hennessy Louis Vuitton solidified its status as the preeminent luxury conglomerate, Chapter 3 of "Mastering Luxury: The Bernard Arnault Chronicles" unravels the artistry behind Bernard Arnault's role as the ultimate curator of dreams. This chapter delves into his distinctive approach to brand management, the delicate balance between tradition and innovation, and the unwavering commitment to quality that became the hallmark of the LVMH portfolio.

The chapter opens with a vivid exploration of Arnault's philosophy on brand curation. Drawing inspiration from the world of fine arts, he viewed each brand within the LVMH portfolio as a masterpiece, deserving meticulous attention and care. The narrative unfolds against the backdrop of iconic Maisons such as Louis Vuitton, Dior, and Moët & Chandon, showcasing how Arnault's keen eye for talent and a deep appreciation for the essence of each brand transformed them into timeless symbols of luxury.

Arnault's approach to brand management is examined through the lens of creative collaborations and strategic partnerships. The chapter delves into the groundbreaking collaborations that redefined luxury, such as the fusion of art and fashion at Louis Vuitton under the creative direction of Marc Jacobs. Arnault's ability to identify and nurture creative geniuses, allowing them the freedom to express their vision while maintaining brand coherence, is a testament to his mastery in orchestrating the symphony of luxury.

The narrative also explores the expansion of the LVMH empire into new territories and markets. Arnault's calculated risk-taking, including the acquisition of Fendi and Sephora, demonstrates his foresight in recognizing trends and capitalizing on emerging consumer preferences. The chapter examines the delicate task of balancing heritage and modernity as LVMH continued to evolve in response to the ever-changing landscape of luxury consumption.

A central theme in this chapter is Arnault's commitment to sustainability and ethical practices. Long before these concepts became buzzwords in the industry, he recognized the importance of responsible business practices, setting a standard for environmental and social responsibility within the luxury sector.

Chapter 3 concludes with LVMH's position as the unrivaled leader in luxury brand management. The reader is left with a profound understanding of Bernard Arnault's role as a curator, shaping the narrative of luxury with a discerning eye, an innovative spirit, and an unyielding commitment to the enduring allure of craftsmanship. This sets the stage for the subsequent chapters, where the narrative will explore the continued evolution of LVMH under Arnault's guidance, as well as the challenges and triumphs that lie ahead in the dynamic world of luxury.

5

The Global Stage

Title: "Luxury Beyond Borders: Bernard Arnault's Global Vision"

As LVMH Moët Hennessy Louis Vuitton entered the late 20th century and embraced the challenges of the 21st, Chapter 4 of "Mastering Luxury: The Bernard Arnault Chronicles" unveils Bernard Arnault's strategic prowess in navigating the global stage. This chapter illuminates the expansion of LVMH's influence across continents, the cultivation of an international clientele, and the dynamic interplay between cultural appreciation and commercial success.

The chapter begins by tracing Arnault's early recognition of the global potential for luxury markets. Fueled by a visionary outlook, he propelled LVMH onto the international stage, understanding that the allure of luxury transcends geographical boundaries. The narrative explores the bold moves that established LVMH as a truly global force, from opening flagship stores in key cities to pioneering the concept of duty-free luxury shopping in airports.

Arnault's diplomatic finesse in managing a diverse portfolio of brands from different cultural backgrounds takes center stage in this chapter. The acquisition of iconic Italian brands such as Bulgari and Fendi showcases his ability to appreciate and preserve the distinct identity of each Maison while fostering a sense of unity within the LVMH family. The reader is immersed in the delicate dance between preserving heritage and embracing a cosmopolitan vision.

A key theme explored in Chapter 4 is Arnault's engagement with emerging markets, particularly in Asia. The narrative unfolds against the backdrop of LVMH's strategic penetration into markets like China and Japan, reflecting Arnault's keen understanding of the cultural nuances that shape luxury preferences. The Maison's adaptation to local tastes, while maintaining an unwavering commitment to craftsmanship, becomes a testament to Arnault's ability to blend tradition with modernity.

The chapter also delves into the challenges encountered in this era of global expansion, from navigating complex international regulations to managing diverse consumer expectations. Arnault's adaptive leadership style and commitment to fostering a culture of innovation within LVMH emerge as critical factors in overcoming these hurdles.

Chapter 4 concludes with LVMH firmly established as a global powerhouse, a testament to Bernard Arnault's vision and leadership. The reader is left with a profound understanding of the intricacies involved in managing a luxury empire on the international stage. This sets the stage for the subsequent chapters, where the narrative will explore the evolving landscape of global luxury, the impact of technology, and the enduring legacy of Bernard Arnault as a trailblazer in the ever-expanding world of opulence.

6

The Digital Revolution

Title: "Luxury in the Digital Age: Bernard Arnault's Visionary Adaptation"

As the 21st century unfolded, the world witnessed the advent of a digital revolution that transformed industries and consumer behaviors. Chapter 5 of "Mastering Luxury: The Bernard Arnault Chronicles" explores Bernard Arnault's foresight in navigating the challenges and opportunities presented by the digital landscape. This chapter delves into LVMH's embrace of technology, the integration of e-commerce into the luxury experience, and Arnault's visionary approach to maintaining exclusivity in an era of accessibility.

The chapter begins by contextualizing the impact of the digital age on the luxury sector. Arnault's recognition of the changing dynamics in consumer behavior, fueled by the rise of online platforms and social media, is explored as a pivotal moment in the narrative. The reader is taken through LVMH's strategic investments in digital infrastructure, from establishing a strong online presence for each Maison to embracing e-commerce without compromising the essence of exclusivity.

Arnault's role as a digital pioneer is illuminated through the Maison's innovative collaborations with tech giants. Whether partnering with leading e-commerce platforms or integrating cutting-edge technology into the retail experience, LVMH's embrace of the digital realm becomes a testament to Arnault's commitment to staying ahead of the curve. The narrative also delves into the challenges of maintaining the allure of luxury in an age of mass accessibility, exploring Arnault's strategic maneuvers to balance accessibility with exclusivity.

A central theme in Chapter 5 is the evolution of marketing and communication strategies within LVMH. Arnault's recognition of the power of storytelling in the digital age is showcased through the Maison's compelling narratives, from behind-the-scenes glimpses of craftsmanship to interactive social media campaigns that engage a global audience. The chapter explores how Arnault leveraged technology not only to reach consumers but also to deepen the emotional connection between the brands and their clientele.

The narrative also unfolds against the backdrop of emerging technologies such as artificial intelligence and augmented reality, exploring how LVMH embraced these innovations to enhance the luxury experience. Arnault's strategic investments in research and development underscore his commitment to marrying traditional craftsmanship with cutting-edge technology.

Chapter 5 concludes with LVMH firmly established as a digital leader in the luxury sector, a testament to Bernard Arnault's ability to adapt and innovate. The reader is left with a profound understanding of the challenges and triumphs of navigating the digital landscape in the pursuit of maintaining the timeless allure of luxury. This sets the stage for the subsequent chapters, where the narrative will explore the continued evolution of LVMH under Arnault's guidance, the impact of geopolitical shifts, and the enduring legacy of a visionary leader in an ever-evolving world.

7

The Resilience of Luxury

Title: "Navigating Challenges: Bernard Arnault's Resilience in the Face of Adversity"

As the world entered an era marked by unprecedented challenges, Chapter 6 of "Mastering Luxury: The Bernard Arnault Chronicles" examines Bernard Arnault's leadership during times of adversity. This chapter unfolds against the backdrop of global economic fluctuations, geopolitical uncertainties, and unforeseen crises, showcasing Arnault's strategic resilience and his ability to steer LVMH through turbulent waters while maintaining the integrity of the luxury experience.

The chapter opens with a retrospective look at the impact of the 2008 financial crisis on the luxury sector. Arnault's strategic maneuvers during this tumultuous period, from maintaining a focus on craftsmanship and quality to exploring new markets, reveal a leader who understood the delicate balance required to weather economic storms without compromising the essence of luxury.

As the narrative progresses, it explores LVMH's response to geopolitical shifts, trade tensions, and the challenges posed by global health crises, including the unprecedented events of the early 2020s. Arnault's swift and decisive actions in adapting business models, redefining supply chains, and leveraging digital platforms underscore his resilience in the face of adversity.

The chapter delves into Arnault's commitment to sustainability as a core component of LVMH's resilience strategy. His proactive stance on environmental responsibility and ethical practices becomes a beacon in an industry facing increasing scrutiny for its impact on the planet. The narrative explores LVMH's initiatives in sustainability, from responsible sourcing of materials to innovative approaches in reducing the environmental footprint of luxury production.

A central theme in Chapter 6 is Arnault's leadership style during times of crisis. The reader gains insights into his ability to inspire and unite teams, fostering a culture of resilience and innovation within LVMH. Arnault's emphasis on talent development, even in challenging times, is explored as a critical factor in the Maison's ability to navigate uncertainty.

The chapter also sheds light on the philanthropic endeavors championed by Arnault and LVMH, showcasing a commitment to social responsibility beyond the realm of luxury. From cultural preservation projects to initiatives supporting healthcare and education, Arnault's vision extends beyond the boardroom, reinforcing the idea that luxury can be a force for positive change in the world.

Chapter 6 concludes with LVMH emerging from challenges stronger and more resilient than ever, a testament to Bernard Arnault's steadfast leadership. The reader is left with a profound understanding of the enduring legacy of a leader who not only shaped the luxury landscape but navigated its complexities with grace and resilience. This sets the stage for the final chapters, where the narrative will explore the future of luxury, the ongoing evolution of LVMH, and the indelible mark left by Bernard Arnault on the world of opulence.

8

The Enduring Legacy

Title: "Beyond Mastery: Bernard Arnault's Timeless Impact on Luxury"

In the final chapter of "Mastering Luxury: The Bernard Arnault Chronicles," the narrative converges on the enduring legacy of a visionary leader whose impact transcends the boundaries of business. This chapter delves into Bernard Arnault's indelible mark on the world of luxury, his philanthropic endeavors, and the ongoing evolution of LVMH as a beacon of innovation and excellence.

The chapter opens by reflecting on Arnault's timeless contributions to the luxury landscape. From reshaping the traditional perceptions of craftsmanship to fostering a culture of continuous innovation, his influence resonates in the very fabric of LVMH. The narrative explores how Arnault's steadfast commitment to quality, coupled with an unwavering pursuit of artistic expression, elevated the Maison to unparalleled heights of global influence.

As the story unfolds, readers gain insights into Arnault's role as a custodian of culture. His efforts to preserve and promote the arts, whether through supporting museums, cultural institutions, or artistic collaborations within the Maison, underscore a commitment to a legacy that extends beyond profit margins. The chapter also explores how Arnault's influence has shaped the broader narrative of luxury, redefining it as a dynamic force capable of transcending commercial realms to become a cultural touchstone.

A central theme in Chapter 7 is Arnault's dedication to nurturing talent and fostering creativity within the Maison. The narrative delves into the symbiotic relationship between the leader and the artistic directors, designers, and artisans who have contributed to the success of LVMH brands. Arnault's ability to recognize and empower creative genius becomes a testament to his role not only as a businessman but also as a patron of the arts.

The chapter also examines Arnault's philanthropic initiatives, exploring the impact of LVMH's contributions to education, healthcare, and environmental causes. From scholarship programs for emerging talent to sustainable practices within the industry, Arnault's commitment to responsible capitalism becomes a defining aspect of his legacy.

As the narrative approaches its conclusion, readers are invited to contemplate the future of luxury and the ongoing evolution of LVMH. Arnault's strategic foresight, coupled with a commitment to timeless values, positions the Maison as a torchbearer for the next generation of luxury consumers.

Chapter 7 concludes with a reflection on Bernard Arnault's enduring legacy. From the genesis of his journey in mastering luxury to the ongoing saga of LVMH's evolution, the reader is left with a profound understanding of a leader whose impact reverberates far beyond the boardrooms of conglomerates. The Bernard Arnault Chronicles stand as a testament to the idea that true mastery in luxury transcends business—it becomes a narrative woven into the fabric of culture, creativity, and the timeless pursuit of excellence.

9

The Future Canvas

Title: "Eternal Innovation: LVMH and the Ever-Evolving Landscape of Luxury"

In the final installment of "Mastering Luxury: The Bernard Arnault Chronicles," Chapter 8 invites readers into the future, exploring the ongoing evolution of LVMH and the dynamic landscape of luxury. This chapter delves into the Maison's continued commitment to innovation, the unfolding role of technology, and the challenges and opportunities that await the next generation of leaders in the world of opulence.

The chapter opens with a retrospective glance at the timeless values ingrained in LVMH's DNA. Bernard Arnault's legacy serves as a guiding light, steering the Maison through a rapidly changing world while upholding the principles of craftsmanship, quality, and artistic expression. Readers are immersed in the Maison's ongoing journey to adapt without compromise, remaining at the forefront of the luxury sector.

A central theme explored in Chapter 8 is the role of technology as a catalyst for innovation. The narrative unfolds against the backdrop of emerging technologies such as artificial intelligence, augmented reality, and blockchain, examining how LVMH continues to integrate these advancements into the luxury experience. The reader is invited to witness the delicate balance between tradition and modernity, as the Maison leverages technology to enhance, rather than replace, the handcrafted essence of luxury.

The chapter also delves into the changing dynamics of consumer behavior and expectations. As the luxury landscape evolves, LVMH remains dedicated to understanding the desires of a new generation of consumers—individuals who value sustainability, authenticity, and unique experiences. Arnault's enduring commitment to staying attuned to these shifts ensures that LVMH remains not only relevant but a trendsetter in the ever-changing world of luxury.

As the narrative progresses, readers gain insights into the collaborative nature of the luxury industry. LVMH's partnerships with other global leaders, from tech giants to cultural institutions, highlight a commitment to cross-disciplinary innovation. The chapter explores how these collaborations contribute to the Maison's ability to shape the narrative of luxury in an interconnected world.

The final chapter also contemplates the succession plan for LVMH and the legacy left by Bernard Arnault. The narrative examines how a new generation of leaders, inspired by Arnault's visionary approach, will carry the torch forward, navigating challenges and embracing opportunities in an era defined by constant change.

Chapter 8 concludes with a forward-looking perspective, inviting readers to ponder the ever-expanding canvas of luxury. As LVMH continues to master the art of innovation, the timeless values instilled by Bernard Arnault stand as a foundation for a future where luxury remains a dynamic, ever-evolving expression of human creativity, craftsmanship, and aspiration.

10

The Unwritten Pages

Title: "Legacy Unfolding: LVMH's Ongoing Journey in Luxury"

As we venture into the final chapter of "Mastering Luxury: The Bernard Arnault Chronicles," Chapter 9 explores the unwritten pages of LVMH's ongoing journey. This chapter unfolds against the backdrop of an ever-changing world, inviting readers to imagine the future of luxury, the continued evolution of LVMH, and the indelible mark that this extraordinary Maison is poised to leave on the global stage.

The chapter begins by contemplating the enduring legacy of Bernard Arnault. His visionary leadership, commitment to excellence, and relentless pursuit of innovation have left an indelible mark on LVMH and the luxury landscape. The reader is immersed in the Maison's dedication to preserving the timeless values instilled by its founder while embracing the imperative for adaptability in an era of unprecedented change.

A central theme explored in Chapter 9 is the intersection of luxury and societal values. As the world grapples with complex challenges, LVMH continues to redefine what it means to be a responsible and sustainable luxury conglomerate. The narrative unfolds against the backdrop of initiatives aimed at addressing environmental concerns, promoting social responsibility, and fostering diversity and inclusion within the industry.

The chapter delves into LVMH's role as a cultural custodian. From supporting the arts to preserving historical landmarks, the Maison's commitment to cultural heritage becomes a cornerstone of its identity. Readers are invited to contemplate how this dedication to culture not only enriches the world but also ensures that the tapestry of luxury is woven with threads of history, creativity, and human connection.

As the narrative progresses, Chapter 9 explores the ever-expanding global footprint of LVMH. From reaching new markets to connecting with diverse audiences, the Maison's ongoing journey reflects a commitment to making luxury accessible without compromising its exclusivity. The chapter invites readers to envision how LVMH will navigate geopolitical shifts, emerging markets, and the dynamic forces shaping the future of the luxury industry.

The chapter also contemplates the role of technology as an enabler of experiences. From virtual fashion shows to immersive retail experiences, the narrative explores how LVMH continues to leverage technology to redefine luxury, connecting with consumers in innovative and meaningful ways while staying true to the artisanal roots of its Maisons.

Chapter 9 concludes by leaving the final pages of the story intentionally unwritten. The Maison's ongoing journey is an ever-unfolding narrative, shaped by the leadership, creativity, and vision of those who carry the torch forward. As readers reach the end of "Mastering Luxury: The Bernard Arnault Chronicles," they are invited to ponder the blank pages that lay ahead—a canvas awaiting the strokes of future leaders, artisans, and visionaries who will continue to shape the legacy of LVMH in the dynamic tapestry of luxury.

11

Epilogue - A Tapestry of Timeless Luxury

Title: "Eternal Elegance: LVMH's Continued Odyssey in Luxury"

In the closing chapter, we gaze upon the epilogue of "Mastering Luxury: The Bernard Arnault Chronicles." This final installment takes us on a reflective journey, celebrating the enduring elegance and perpetual innovation that define LVMH's legacy in the world of luxury.

The chapter opens with a retrospective glance at the tapestry woven throughout the preceding pages. From the genesis of Bernard Arnault's visionary leadership to the Maison's constant evolution in response to global shifts, the narrative encapsulates the essence of LVMH's timeless journey.

A central theme in the epilogue is the concept of eternal elegance. It explores how LVMH, under the stewardship of successive leaders inspired by Arnault's legacy, continues to define and refine the epitome of sophistication. The reader is immersed in the Maison's commitment to craftsmanship, artistic expression, and a pursuit of beauty that transcends temporal boundaries.

As the narrative unfolds, we witness the evolution of luxury as a living, breathing entity. The epilogue contemplates how LVMH navigates the ever-changing desires of a discerning clientele. The Maison's ability to stay attuned to the pulse of societal values, emerging trends, and technological advancements ensures that its offerings remain not only relevant but anticipatory of the desires of generations to come.

A significant aspect explored in the epilogue is the interplay between heritage and innovation. LVMH's ongoing dedication to preserving the traditions and stories that define its Maisons harmonizes with a commitment to push the boundaries of what luxury can be. Readers are invited to reflect on how this delicate dance between the past and the future continues to shape the narrative of LVMH.

The chapter also contemplates the global impact of LVMH as a cultural ambassador. From the cobblestone streets of Paris to the bustling markets of emerging economies, the Maison's influence resonates. The epilogue explores how LVMH's commitment to cultural preservation, diversity, and responsible business practices solidifies its role as a beacon in the luxury landscape.

As readers reach the final pages, they are invited to reflect on the indelible mark left by Bernard Arnault and the ongoing saga of LVMH. The epilogue symbolizes not just an end but a continuum—a commitment to perpetuating the artistry, innovation, and elegance that define luxury in its most exquisite form.

In the closing lines, "Mastering Luxury: The Bernard Arnault Chronicles" acknowledges that the story is not static. Instead, it lives on through the unwritten chapters, awaiting the pens of those who will continue to shape the legacy of LVMH—an eternal odyssey in the art of mastering luxury.

12

A Glimpse into Tomorrow

Title: "The Future Unveiled: LVMH and the Next Chapter in Luxury"

As we venture into Chapter 11 of "Mastering Luxury: The Bernard Arnault Chronicles," the narrative shifts its focus towards the horizon, offering readers a tantalizing glimpse into the future of LVMH and the unfolding narrative of luxury. This chapter delves into the ever-evolving landscape of the industry, the challenges and opportunities that lie ahead, and the role that LVMH is poised to play in shaping the next chapter of opulence.

The chapter begins by examining the dynamic forces that will shape the future of luxury. From shifting consumer behaviors and evolving tastes to geopolitical influences and advancements in technology, the reader is immersed in the complexities that will define the path forward. A key theme is the Maison's adaptability, exploring how LVMH anticipates and navigates the unpredictable currents of a changing world.

A central focus in Chapter 11 is the role of sustainability in shaping the future of luxury. As global awareness of environmental and social issues continues to grow, the narrative explores how LVMH leads the charge in adopting eco-friendly practices, supporting ethical sourcing, and contributing to a more sustainable luxury landscape. The reader is invited to contemplate how these efforts will not only meet current expectations but also set new standards for responsible luxury.

The chapter also delves into the evolving definition of exclusivity in an era of increased accessibility. With the rise of digital platforms and changing consumer expectations, the narrative explores how LVMH continues to redefine the concept of exclusivity without diluting the essence of luxury. The reader is prompted to envision how the Maison will maintain a delicate balance between widespread accessibility and the coveted allure of exclusivity.

A significant aspect of Chapter 11 is the exploration of emerging markets and the ever-expanding global reach of luxury. As new economies rise and consumer demographics shift, the narrative contemplates how LVMH will navigate and contribute to the diverse tapestry of luxury experiences across the world. The reader is invited to envision the Maison's role in shaping the aspirations and desires of a new generation of luxury enthusiasts.

The chapter also examines the ongoing integration of technology into the luxury experience. From virtual reality shopping to personalized digital interactions, the narrative explores how LVMH embraces technological advancements to enhance the customer journey while maintaining the essence of handcrafted excellence.

As Chapter 11 unfolds, readers are encouraged to reflect on the leadership that will guide LVMH into the future. The narrative contemplates how successive leaders will draw inspiration from the legacy of Bernard Arnault while infusing their own visions into the ever-evolving narrative of luxury.

In the concluding lines of this chapter, the reader is left with a sense of anticipation and excitement—an invitation to witness the unrivaled elegance and innovation that will unfold in the next chapters of LVMH's remarkable journey in mastering luxury.

13

The Everlasting Elegance

Title: "Legacy in Bloom: LVMH's Timeless Odyssey in Luxury Continues"

In the concluding chapter of "Mastering Luxury: The Bernard Arnault Chronicles," we turn our gaze to the enduring elegance and the perpetually evolving odyssey of LVMH in the world of luxury. Chapter 12 serves as both a reflection and a prologue—a celebration of the Maison's timeless legacy and a contemplation of the chapters yet to be written.

The chapter opens with a profound acknowledgment of the indelible mark left by LVMH on the global stage of luxury. From the illustrious halls of fashion to the effervescent world of champagne, the Maison's influence is a testament to its commitment to excellence, craftsmanship, and the unwavering pursuit of beauty.

A central theme explored in Chapter 12 is the concept of enduring elegance. As the narrative contemplates the future, it delves into how LVMH's commitment to timeless values—values woven into the very fabric of its Maisons—serves as a compass guiding the Maison through the ever-shifting currents of the luxury landscape. The reader is invited to witness the perpetual refinement of elegance, an art form that remains relevant across epochs.

The chapter also reflects on the evolution of luxury as a cultural force. LVMH's role as a custodian of art, heritage, and innovation becomes a beacon in an ever-changing world. The narrative explores how the Maison's dedication to preserving cultural narratives and fostering creativity ensures that luxury is not merely a commodity but an immersive experience—a journey into the heart of human expression.

A significant aspect of Chapter 12 is the interplay between tradition and innovation. The narrative contemplates how LVMH, rooted in a legacy of artisanal craftsmanship, continues to embrace the cutting edge of technology, setting new standards for modern luxury. The reader is prompted to envision the fusion of heritage and progress as a symphony that defines the very essence of the Maison.

As the narrative progresses, the chapter contemplates the role of LVMH in shaping societal values. With a spotlight on sustainability, diversity, and ethical practices, the Maison's commitment to responsible luxury becomes a cornerstone of its identity. The reader is invited to reflect on how these values will not only resonate with contemporary audiences but also transcend time, shaping the future narrative of opulence.

The concluding lines of Chapter 12 echo a sentiment of eternal optimism. The reader is left with a sense of anticipation—a recognition that the story of LVMH is an ever-unfolding saga, and its legacy will continue to blossom and evolve in ways that captivate the hearts and imaginations of generations yet to come. As the book closes, it leaves the door ajar for the Maison to continue its timeless odyssey in mastering the art of luxury.

14

Summary

"Mastering Luxury: The Bernard Arnault Chronicles" is a comprehensive exploration of the journey undertaken by Bernard Arnault and LVMH Moët Hennessy Louis Vuitton in shaping the landscape of luxury. Across twelve chapters, the narrative unfolds from Arnault's early years, his strategic acquisitions, and the formation of LVMH, to the Maison's global expansion, the impact of technology, and its resilience during times of adversity.

The book delves into the visionary leadership of Bernard Arnault, portraying him as a trailblazer who mastered the delicate balance between tradition and innovation. It emphasizes Arnault's role as a curator of dreams, orchestrating a portfolio of prestigious brands under the LVMH umbrella. The narrative explores the evolution of luxury in the digital age, detailing LVMH's embrace of technology while preserving the essence of exclusivity.

Chapters dedicated to challenges highlight Arnault's resilience, adaptability, and commitment to sustainability. The narrative also underscores his philanthropic endeavors and the integration of responsible business practices within the luxury sector. The global expansion of LVMH, its impact on emerging markets, and the delicate dance between preserving heritage and embracing modernity are recurring themes.

The later chapters anticipate the future, envisioning LVMH's role in the ever-evolving luxury landscape. The narrative contemplates sustainability, the integration of technology, and the ongoing commitment to timeless values. The book concludes with a sense of perpetual elegance, leaving the door open for the Maison to continue its legacy as a beacon of innovation and excellence in the art of mastering luxury.

www.ingramcontent.com/pod-product-compliance
Lightning Source LLC
LaVergne TN
LVHW020538160826
845677LV00015B/4135
9785685014023